THE DIGNITY
AND
VOCATION
OF
WOMEN

Mulieris Dignitatem

Together! recognizes the generous contributions of the following
who have made this publication possible:

Sister Mary Jeremiah, O.P., STD.

Genevieve Kineke

Paul and Libbie Sellors

THE DIGNITY

AND

VOCATION

OF

WOMEN

Leader's Manual

Together!

Together!

Together, Inc.
3205 Roosevelt Street NE • St Anthony MN 55418
www.togetherinc.net
Copyright © 2007,2005,2002,1998

ISBN 978-1-933463-11-7
ISBN 1-933463-11-2

THE DIGNITY AND VOCATION OF WOMEN
LEADER'S MANUAL

TABLE OF CONTENTS

Table of Contents v

Introduction 1

About Together! 2
    Mission 2
    Means 2
    Audience 2
    Objectives 2

Set up steps 2

Preparing for Sessions 2
    An Effective Method of Preparation 4
    Handling Uncomfortable Situations 5

Leader's Guide 7

SESSION ONE 9
    Articles 1-3 9

SESSION TWO 13
    Articles 4-5 13

SESSION THREE 17
    Articles 6-8 17

SESSION FOUR 21
    Articles 9-11 21

SESSION FIVE 25
    Articles 12-16 25

SESSION SIX 29
    Articles 17-19 29

SESSION SEVEN 33
    Articles 20-22 33

SESSION EIGHT 37
    Articles 23-27 37

SESSION NINE 41

Articles 28-30 41

SESSION TEN 45
Articles 30-31 45

Leader's Evaluation 51

Leader's Manual

Introduction

This manual has been written with you in mind, to be a tool for you as you undertake an important mission. It will provide you with the information and methodology you need to lead a group of men and/or women to a greater understanding of the plan that God has for each one of us.

Christ has chosen you to do this work because you are eager to do something for him. For some, taking on this role of leadership will not be a great challenge, while for others it may seem to be something quite extraordinary. Regardless, keep in mind that not only does Christ call, but at the same time he gives you his grace to be effective in what he asks you to do for him.

So that you can be most effective in the task at hand, we are providing in this manual the methodology to get you going and keep you on track. Keep in mind that the goal is to journey with your group through this program letting the words of the author speak for themselves. As apostles of Christ, you will benefit both spiritually and intellectually from this experience. Be generous in leading the group. Through your humility and charity, you will help them see the wisdom of God. In turn, they will want to cultivate that same spirit within their own relationships.

Be sure to read through this manual. Understand how the program has been laid out. Encourage others to see it as a gift through which they will come to understand how God has created each of us. Pray for them and encourage them to make this a special journey. The methodology, as outlined in this manual, will guide you from the start.

May God bless you in your work!

Paul and Libbie Sellors

About Together!

Mission

Together! will provide participants the means, through programs of study, to recognize the gifts they have received from God, to learn more about their Catholic Faith and the relationship of that Faith to daily life. Participants will enrich their relationship with those around them, improve their relationship with God, and share ideas with others of like mind.

Means

Together! provides programs by which participants in small groups or individually can understand how the constant teaching of the Church enriches daily life and indeed strengthens marriage and family against the influences of the world. These programs are meant to be a simple practical study based on the teaching documents of the Church documents which are easily understood through the Together! methodology. Although in most programs the complete document is provided in the Study Guide, these programs are not meant to be heavy academic studies.

Audience

Together! fosters in husbands, wives, fathers, mothers, singles and young adults a practical social, psychological, moral and religious formation so they may realize more fully their mission in daily life within family, Church and society.

Objectives

- Shed light and gain insight on ways to meet the need for Christ and the Church in daily life.
- Spread the teaching of the Catholic Church,
- Assist parents in molding a strong family structure.
- Assist young adults in making correct choices in choosing marriage or religious life.
- Promote harmony between husband and wife.
- Provide parents with tools to form mature, responsible young adults.

Set up steps

- Select the location (home, parish hall, school, community center, etc.) where the group will meet.
- If there is more than one Leader, determine what responsibility each will have.
- Establish the meeting calendar, with input from the group, beginning with the first session and then for the anticipated duration of the program. Meeting every two weeks is recommended. Each group maintains its own schedule that is dependent on the meeting place and the participants' personal schedules.

Preparing for Sessions

In preparing for the first group session, it is important that you have a clear understanding of the program and all aspects of a group session. Please read the following section carefully to become familiar with the program.

Materials Needed: In addition to your Leaders Guide and document to be studied, you should have with you a Catholic Bible or Missal as well as a copy of the *Catechism of the Catholic Church*.

1. Prepare each lesson from the "Leader's Guide" before each session. It will be helpful to use the questions to go through each session's study material before looking at the answers. If the parish or diocese provides preparatory sessions, take advantage of them!.

    Note: The answers provided in the Leader's Guide are meant to be a springboard for stimulating active discussion or as a means to round out discussion.

2. <u>Do not read the answers</u> to the participants from your guide. In advance, read and digest the contents, drawing on the key points. Then inject these points into the discussion.

    If you think it would be helpful to the group, you may wish to draw from your own experiences or those of your parents and family. These personal experiences can truly illustrate the truths of the faith or show how our faith is a part of everyday life. However, a word of caution: we sometimes see situations where leaders have used a lengthy personal story to illustrate each question which didn't allow time to finish the session, nor the participants time to ask questions, discuss a point or speak of their own personal experiences.

3. Practice being a good listener. Keep your eyes on the speaker and respond to what he or she has said either by a nod or a verbal response.

4. Keep to the session plan, follow the given time allotment. While humility is an invaluable virtue, the Leader does have, and must exercise his or her authority to bring the main points of the session back into focus.

    Make sure that if the discussion should wander off track that you bring it back on track again quickly. Co-leaders must work together as a team to provide each other support in returning the discussion to the lesson. When the intent is to continue discussing a point, then just stating the question in another way is an effective method. When the discussion has completely moved away from the subject and needs to end, then simply summarize the answer to the question before moving on with the next question. Always be pleasant and tactful! With some discussions that get off track, it might be helpful to ask the person if "we could talk about that afterwards so we can move on."

    Often there will be one or two in the group who will need some extra attention to be drawn into discussion. Usually the discussion develops with the extroverts in the group. Then the Leader can casually ask one who has been non-communicative what he or she could add to that point of discussion. Keep mental note of who stays silent and needs help. Ask open-ended questions, that is, ones that must be answered with something more than a simple yes or no. Ask such questions as "How would this effect you?" or "What could you do in that situation?"

5.   Co-leaders must work together to keep the session on time and on track. It is considerate to the participants who have baby-sitters or limited time to attend. It simply makes good sense to start the meeting on time and end it on time while covering all the material. If a person wants to discuss a particular point further, ask to do so after the session has ended. In that way he or she can get the help needed and that allows others to leave on-time with all the material covered.

An Effective Method of Preparation

- Look at the main ideas within your material. Start with the questions to see what the participants are expected to comprehend.

- Write those ideas down.

- Then read the material looking for your understanding of those main points.

- Be able to state in your own words those main ideas by the time you begin each session.

- Make sure that the "main" points have been covered and understood by the participants.

- Take a mental inventory as your group goes through the session. Ask yourself if these ideas were covered. Did they "get it?"

- This is important because one session builds upon the next - if they miss an important point it is difficult for them to accept or understand the following points. There are other methods of study but this is one that is easy, very effective, and efficient.

- Look at the program and ask yourself, what is its goal or the charism

- Always back up your study and presentation with prayer to the Holy Spirit. You are doing His work.

Handling Uncomfortable Situations

Have you ever been in a group where someone has made a particular comment and the air suddenly crackles with electricity? You may have experienced 'the great silence' where you can hear a pin drop. On the other hand, maybe everyone starts talking at once in shock over a comment someone has made. What are you to do? Here are some basic principles used to defuse or to prevent some of these uncomfortable situations.

Remember that an underlying principle is that you are the role model for your participants. If you are charitable and enthusiastic about the teachings of the Church, the participants will reflect your enthusiasm and charity. They will grow in their friendship with God, enrich their relationship with their spouse and children and share positive ideas with other parents. We are there to heal families, not to tear them apart by judging and condemning the members.

Here are some tips that might help you:
- Try to use humor effectively, without being frivolous. Occasionally groups exhibit a need for laughter and light hearted joking to release built up tension which can sometimes lead to confrontations.

- Let Christ be your example. Christ was often harsh when dealing with the attitudes or actions of groups of people (Pharisees) but showed individuals great understanding and compassion, while also calling them to a change of heart.

- Never say anything to them that is condemning. That would immediately close the door to any open discussion. Remember that we are not there to judge but to bring the truths of the faith. As Christ does, see others as souls in need and accept their strengths and weaknesses. That attitude will promote understanding and motivation which will, in turn, establish trust with the other person.

- Develop empathy for others, the ability to tune into what others are subjectively experiencing and see the world through their eyes. Resist the urge to offer quick advice or give "pat" answers. Be an active listener by reflecting back to the person that we're listening to, what you just heard him or her say, we hear them saying, consciously or unconsciously. For example, suppose that someone were to share that his brother is going through a divorce, adding that he lives far away and wishes he could be closer to him. You could reflect back what you hear him saying, "It sounds like you're struggling with the fact of your brother is going through a divorce and you wish you lived closer so you could help her him." The person will usually respond with a nonverbal nod or grunt or will correct the misinterpretation. The result is that he remains open to further discussion and you have a better understanding of the situation.

- Always be genuine, authentic. Therefore:
  - Do not pretend to accept what someone is saying or sharing when internally you

are not accepting it.
- You could say, "I would be uncomfortable with that"
- Don't rely on comments or behaviors aimed at winning approval
- Avoid hiding behind the role as the leader — dynamism is called for
- When you are authentic, you are a model to the participants. You will inspire them to be real in their reactions.
- Being natural and sincere are indispensable conditions for the apostle to attract others.
- Respect for others is shown by what the leader does, not simply by what he says.

To sum up some attitudes and actions that show respect:
- Avoid critical judgments — Avoid labeling actions and persons
- Look beyond self-imposed or other-imposed labels
- Express warmth and support that are honestly felt — Be genuine and risk being you
- Recognize the rights of others to be different from you

In Conclusion:
This program is well planned and has proven successful. Do not try to change it! Be sure to follow the format given in this Leader's Manual. Pay attention to details. Be sure to use your manual as a reference often.

People value the fact that they can count on the authenticity of the program. Others will receive the truth if you are faithful to the approved specified format and content.

THE DIGNITY
AND
VOCATION
OF
WOMEN

Leader's Guide

SESSION ONE

Mulieris Dignitatem
Articles 1-3

Our study of this Apostolic Letter, "On the Dignity and Vocation of Women," is divided under four major headings to illustrate woman's relationship to Jesus Christ.

Women and Jesus Christ -- Eternal Word of God

1. Pope John Paul II quotes from the closing message of the Second Vatican Council in his opening paragraph:
    > "The hour is coming, in fact has come, when the vocation of women is being acknowledged in its fullness, the hour in which women acquire in the world an influence, an effect and a power never hitherto achieved. That is why, at this moment when the human race is undergoing so deep a transformation, women imbued with a spirit of the Gospel can do so much to aid humanity in not falling."[1]

    Q. Considering the state of the family, why is the Gospel message so important to mankind today?

    A. The Pope notes in his apostolic exhortation, *Familiaris Consortio,* ("The Church in the Modern World") that "the family is the object of numerous forces that seek to destroy it or in some way to deform it."[2] Both the nature of marital love and the very definition of "family" are contested. Since the well-being of each generation is "intimately tied to the good of the family,"[3] it becomes evident that, without this key institution to nurture and safeguard them, many persons are more vulnerable to lies, alienated from authentic love, and unable to benefit from lasting relationships. As they turn to materialism or hedonism for the consolation and support that are otherwise missing, their confusion deepens. The Gospel gives us Christ as the Way, the Truth and the Life. It gives us our motivation and purpose in life, defining our part in God's creation, and showing us how to respond to God. Ultimately, the Gospel message allows us the opportunity to receive God's gift of grace and to use it to transform our families, our friends and all of society.

---

[1] *Address of Pope Paul VI to Women* (December 8, 1965).

[2] *Familiaris Consortio*, par. 3.

[3] *Ibid.*

2.   Q. **Identify some of the areas of confusion in the role of women in today's society.**

     A.   Some of the areas or questions referred to may be:
- What do we mean by equality?
- Is it appropriate for women to take part in military combat?
- Why *can't* women be priests?
- Is today's society unjust to women?
- What is the ultimate vocation of women?
- Are mothers and fathers interchangeable?
- Is motherhood itself demeaning to women?
- Are modesty and chivalry old-fashioned?
- Why should women cooperate with men?

3.   The Holy Father recognizes the many areas of confusion in society, and, in writing this document, wishes to accomplish three objectives:

     a.   to show esteem for women,

     b.   to consider the excellence of the feminine genius

     c.   to address modern feminism.

     Q. **What were the original feminists trying to address? Were there inherent injustices in various cultures before the sexual revolution began in the West?**

     A.   As weary as many are of the sexual revolution, there were inherent injustices that some women (and men) sought to address through feminism. Various parts of the world discouraged education for girls, and legitimate professions were often closed to women. Laws often excluded women from voting, managing their affairs or even making legal claims in their own right. Subtle double standards often inhibited the options of women compared to men, and the worst of cultures blatantly held that women were inferior to men.

4.   Q. **Why is it important to look at what the Church is saying about the true dignity of women? What ethos or credibility does the Church have in this regard?**

     A.   The Catholic Church has consistently stressed the fundamental equality of men and women, while respecting their innate differences. The teachings of recent popes (since Pius XII) have acknowledged women's importance and noted that their full potentialities have not yet been made clear. In addition to progress, the Church has expressed great concerns about the excesses of radical feminism, which rejects certain truths about human sexuality. Before we can understand, appreciate and implement women's appropriate and active presence in the Church and society, we must first understand her fundamental dignity and vocation. Through Christ and His Church, we learn what it means to be fully human. The Church has 2,000 years of experience and reflection, as well as the promised guidance of the Holy Spirit, to help us come to the fullness of truth.

5. Q. **Why does the Pope begin by speaking of Mary and the Marian Year?**

    A. It is a means of transition. This letter is based on what he wrote in his encyclical, *Redemptoris Mater*. Mary is the Mother and Woman to whom all people have been entrusted by Christ. Since Mary was a woman and shared intimately in Christ's redemptive mission, she is a model and guide for women in a special way for living their Christian vocation. From the beginning, a woman, and women in general, have a special part to play in God's plan of salvation. Both the encyclical on Mary and this document on women were written during the Marian Year of 1987-1988.[4]

6. Chapter 2 of *Mulieris Dignitatem* returns to themes discussed in *Redemptoris Mater*; God sent forth His Son born of a woman. The culmination and fullness of God's self-revelation is the Incarnation of the Eternal Word as a human being. God becomes what we are so that we might become what He is. God unites Himself with humanity through Mary's "Fiat," so we can share in the Divine Life of the Trinity.

    Q. **In what ways can we respond to so great a gift?**

    A. We should do everything possible to keep that divine life within us by our total acceptance of that gift and the responsibility that it implies. We are called to remain in the state of grace through prayer, frequent reception of the Sacraments – especially the Eucharist and confession, and by sharing what we have freely received with others – including extended family, neighbors, coworkers, and people we encounter only briefly. We should join our prayers to those of the universal Church, and in this way imitate Mary who was called to bear humbly Christ to the world.

7. Continuing with the themes of *Redemptoris Mater*: The Eternal Word of the Father became man, born of a woman in the fullness of time. Mary is the *Theotokos*, a Greek term meaning God-bearer, meaning that she is indeed the

---

[4] Pope John Paul II repeats this importance of Mary for women in his book, *Crossing the Threshold*, pp. 216-217.

Mother of God. Mary's new name, "Full of Grace," reveals both a supernatural reality and a vocation. She has a special role in the redemptive work of her Son. To serve is to reign.

Q. How does the fullness of time reveal the extraordinary dignity of the Woman?

A. A woman is to be found at the center of this salvific event – Mary.

- The Woman represents *all humanity* not only women. All humanity is destined for union with God.
- The unity of God with all humanity takes place initially in a way that can belong only to a woman, who received the love of the Bridegroom in a fruitful embrace, bearing life for the kingdom.
- Mary is not a passive tool, but responds with her whole free will. Therefore, she shares in this event with all her personal and feminine qualities.
- The Mother of God takes part in an interpersonal event or dialogue. She is the archetype of all women as well as the Universal Church, the spotless bride. God's action truly hinges on her reply to His invitation.

SESSION TWO

Mulieris Dignitatem
Articles 4-5

1. In Session 1, we learned that the "fullness of time manifests the extraordinary dignity of the woman." Christ becoming man through a woman imparts great dignity — on both women and all of humanity, whose likeness He assumed in the flesh. *The dignity of women is both a fact and a vocation.* It is a fact imparted by Christ's Incarnation; and giving birth to Christ is the perfection of what is feminine, placing motherhood at the foundation of the woman's vocation. It is an active characteristic, indicating the call to receive, develop and giving birth to Christ in the hearts of people.

   The fullness of feminine holiness is modeled by Mary, who — being "full of grace" — is the person most united to God. As a woman, this high dignity reflects upon all other women who follow her example. *The dignity and vocation of each woman are found in union with God.*

   Q. How can you be a spiritual mother, giving birth to Christ in the hearts of the people in your daily life?

   A. One must know Christ in order to give Him to others. We can know Him through the Sacraments, Holy Scripture, through embracing our sufferings, prayer, self-denial, and through the virtuous people in our lives. Developing personal holiness brings peace, goodness, hope, optimism, strength, helpfulness, and love of Christ to others. Never underestimate the value of witnessing a holy, Christian life.

   Some practical ways can be to support your friends and family through their personal trials, bringing them encouragement and care through sickness and death, as well as through their joys, such as childbirth or success. Consider even the importance of a sincere smile for co-workers, neighbors, and a child who returns home from school. Your treatment of his or her friends can have a big influence on them and on your child.

2. There is another characteristic or special quality of women pointed out by the Holy Father. It is expressed by Mary's response, "I am the handmaid of the Lord."

   Q. Why is "handmaiden" such a charged word that alienates many women?

   A. Centuries of poorly constructed cultures reflected the fall from grace in the Garden of Eden which undermined the original unity of man and woman. God said to the woman, "I will greatly multiply your pain in childbearing; in pain you shall bring forth children, yet your desire shall be for your husband, and he shall rule over you" (*Gn* 3:16). When an abuse of the man's greater strength is imbedded in law and culture, the woman finds herself at a tremendous disadvantage, often resulting in an estranged form of subservience. Thus, women instinctively shy away from the possibility of becoming "doormats" or "stepping stones," and resent situations in which they feel degraded by law or action. When a Christian woman is initially introduced to the essence of her vocation — as handmaiden, the negative associations with such exploitation can make her recoil until she understands the gift of service associated with Christ and His command of mutual submission.

3. Q. **How does Mary's understanding of her vocation model humility to all her children in the faith?**

    A. In article 5, Mary expresses a complete awareness of being the creature of a loving and generous God. Jesus, her Son, explained that He "came not to be served but to serve," and His humble service redeemed the world. Mary shared in His saving service from the very beginning. Jesus said the greatest in the Kingdom is the one who serves, because service bears a royal dignity. The humility attached to service is the opposite of the pride of the fallen angels, who insisted that they would not serve (*non serviam*) in such a Kingdom. Likewise, it turns the pride of our first parents on its head. Authentic love seeks to serve the beloved, and in that way, our God constantly serves us. A special quality of woman is loving service of others (cf., June 25, 1995 *Letter to Women*, Articles 10 & 11).

4. Q. **How does the Christian vision of service differ from the world's view?**

    A. The secular world does not always value self-giving service. More often the world tells us to "do your own thing," to "stick up for your rights" or "don't let others take advantage." The Christian view appreciates self-denial, prioritizing the needs of others out of love. The Christian imitates Christ, Who emptied Himself and gave His life for others. In this light Mary was His first and most perfect disciple.

5. Q. **How do you view service? Is it hard or easy? Enriching or impoverishing?**

    A. Answers will vary. Reflect upon how you perform your daily duties. Look carefully at each task to see if what motivates you is positive or negative. Of course the best motivation is to perform any activity for the love of God and neighbor. If necessary, make a resolution to work with joy and consider service as a way to serve God through family, neighbors and coworkers.

6. Q. **How should the authentically feminine response differ from the feminist reaction that has been widely manifest in the last 40 years?**

    A. In the opening session, we discussed how societal arrangements in the last 100 years were often unfair and degrading to women. Many women simply wanted equality under the law, access to jobs and education, and an end to a sexual double standard. Radical feminism took the initial goals further in ways that blur the distinctions between men and women and undermine the rights of the unborn. The Catholic response should be a careful balance of respect for authentic differences between the sexes without degradation of either at the hands of the other; and, most importantly, the authentic feminine response would incorporate a respect for both service and motherhood.

Mulieris Dignitatem
Articles 6-8

Image and Likeness

1. Q. **What is the basic Christian anthropology? And in what ways are humans in the "image and likeness" of God?**

    A. "God created man in his own image, in the image of God He created him; male and female he created them" (*Gn* 1:27 – the first creation story). The human being is the peak of the visible created world, and man and woman are human to an equal degree, share a mutual beginning and are called to collaborate in their dominion over the earth.

    God is a personal God and every human person is created in His image and likeness. The human person "images" God by being rational, free, capable of knowing and loving God. Humans are rational creatures and have been given dominion (share God's authority) over the rest of the visible world.

2. Q. **The second creation story gives further insights into our understanding of the human person. Discuss some of those insights.**

    A. The creation of the woman from the side of man indicates her essential relationship to him. It reveals the fundamental equality between man and woman and God's plan for their collaboration and communion. They are called to form a "unity of the two," being companions and helpers to one another. The Judeo-Christian tradition sees this as the institution of marriage at the very beginning of creation. This union is "indispensable" for the transmission of new life, and their joint concern creates an ongoing safeguard for the well-being of their offspring. In that union, they are called "to exist mutually for the other."

3. Man was alone until the creation of woman. Because the Trinity is three Persons in one God, human beings living in a mutual self-giving relationship reflect the "image and likeness" of the triune God.

    *   The man and woman are called to live in a communion of love. The great commandment of Jesus is, "Love one another" (*Jn* 13). Scripture also says, "God is love" (*1 Jn* 4:16).
    *   The man and woman, as individuals, image God as free, rational beings. But also man and woman together, as a unity, image God in the communion of love.

Q. **Discuss specific ways that sacramental marriage draws on the Trinity as a guide for life-giving love.**

A. There should be a tremendous number of examples, which reflect that couples who ground their marriages in prayer enjoy the guidance of the Holy Spirit, follow the example of the generosity of the Son, and find their meaning in the Father, from Whom all families take their name (cf. *Eph* 3:14-15). The reciprocal love of the Father for the Son and Son for the Father "breathes" the Holy Spirit in the same way that the mutual love of man and woman breathes forth new life — usually in children, but often in other signs of love, service, and gifts to the world.

The Pope quotes *Gaudium et Spes* as saying there is a "certain likeness" between the union of the Trinity and that of human persons.[5] Each divine Person within the Trinity pours Itself out in love for the others. Because human persons are created in this divine image, they are fully themselves when they image (reflect) that Trinitarian self-giving. A person fully finds himself only through a "sincere gift of self." Another way of saying this is, "the person exists for the other to become a gift." Pope John Paul II refers to this self-gift as the "spousal" character of the relationship between persons.

4. **Q.** **Even outside of marriage, consider how giving yourself to another enabled you to be more of a person: helped you grow in self-realization and self-discovery?**

A. The answers will vary, and many fine examples could be found in the formative years when many began to leave behind the natural selfishness of youth. The lessons of generous love — coping with illness, enduring hardships, finding that material possessions weren't as important in the long run as relationships and memories — are powerful and may be shared by the participants.

5. The principle of analogy is a very important theological concept. It is the comparison of two things that are similar, yet different. This principle, used in Scripture, helps us speak of God Who is totally beyond us and of Whom we can really know very little. The similarities help our limited minds to grasp infinite ideas, and yet the limits of the analogies must always be kept in mind so that we don't limit the truths of God.

Q. **In speaking of biblical anthropomorphism, the Pope refers to the principle of analogy. Using examples from Scripture, in what ways is God analogous to a father and in what ways is God analogous to**

---

[5] *Gaudium et spes*, 24.

a mother?

A. In many passages God's love is presented as the "masculine" love of the bridegroom and father (cf. *Hosea* 11:1-4; *Jer* 3:4-19), and Jesus always addressed God as His Father. Parables such as the prodigal son likened God to a generous father. For divine motherhood, Scripture gives the examples: "But Zion said, 'The Lord has forsaken me, my Lord has forgotten me.' 'Can a woman forget her sucking child, that she should have no compassion on the son of her womb? Even these may forget, yet I will not forget you'" (*Is* 49:14-15); "As one whom his mother comforts, so will I comfort you; you shall be comforted in Jerusalem" (*Is* 66: 13); "Like a child quieted at its mother's breast; like a child that is quieted is my soul. O Israel, hope in the Lord" (*Ps* 131:2-3). God's care for His people is shown to be like that of a mother, who "has carried" humanity, and in particular, his Chosen People, within his own womb; giving birth with suffering, then nourishing and comforting it (cf. *Is* 42:14; 46:3-4).

6. The most important attribute of God after that of His very essence (being "love") is that love is generative by nature.

Q. **How does "eternal generation," which belongs to the inner life of God differ from the masculine and feminine ways of generating life?**

A. While biblical anthropomorphism tries to help us understand the ways that man is analogous to God, we must remember that God generates with neither masculine nor feminine qualities. His way is, by nature, totally divine and has no bodily properties, since "God is spirit" (*Jn* 4:24).

7. Q. **Why do you think that God would ask us to consider him "Father" when by nature He is not masculine? What happens when we call God "Mother?"**

A. While we can never know the mind of God perfectly, there must have been a compelling reason why He asked to be called "Father," and the reason can be deduced from both our understanding of "fatherhood" and the way people arrange their perceptions of the created world.

1. In considering the way that humans reproduce, the father is completely separate from his creation, although intimately concerned for the well-being of his offspring. There is never confusion concerning the fact that the father is other than the child. The mother, on the other hand, is physically tied to the child and this tangible communion often continues years after birth, due to the shared flesh, the years of nursing, and the ensuing physical bond.

The mother is the child's world — his very sanctuary for years — and it is her vocation to introduce him to his father and build bridges.

2. Interestingly, pagan religions that worship a feminine deity are naturally pantheistic, because the goddess becomes entwined with her creation in the ways that mothers are physically entwined with their own offspring. Thus, the earth is the goddess, or the tree is worshiped as part of her "essence."

3. As we unfold the mysteries of creation and move towards a nuptial understanding of God's creation, with the understanding of Christ as Bridegroom laying down His life for His beloved, it leaves room for the feminine paradigm of Bride, who is to be found in the Virgin Mary, Holy Mother Church, and the life of each woman. "You cannot have God for your Father if you do not have the Church for your mother" (Saint Cyprian, d. 258).

Mulieris Dignitatem
Articles 9-11

Eve - Mary

1. Having explained that man is in the "image and likeness" of God, Who is perfectly good, sin is explained as a "non-likeness," a breach in the relationship between God and creation. Sin is explained as opposition, or negation to the plan of God.

    Q. If freedom is the ability to choose the good, and sin is the abuse of that freedom, how has the modern understanding of "freedom" been so corrupted?

    A. Man rejected God's gift of supernatural happiness. Despite the "call to both man and woman to share in the intimate life of God Himself," they used their free will to sin, trying to attain by their own power — on their own terms — what God had actually willed: that they be like God. Freedom, in modern parlance, is actually "license" which simply acknowledges that humans have free will, the ability to choose. When one chooses badly (outside of God's will) this desire becomes destructive, selfish, and perverted, resulting in a disruption of communion — both with God and with others. Such "freedom" is actually slavery to sin, and ends in death. Instead of being "like God," in sinning they lose their likeness to God.

2. **Q. What are the consequences of Original Sin?**

    A. There are eight consequences which are disruptions of unity:
    *   between God and His creatures
    *   between the man and the woman
    *   within the created world
    *   obscuring and diminishing the image and likeness of God in humans
    *   "Your desire shall be for your husband and He shall rule over you"
    *   Man dominates woman instead of offering a "sincere gift of self"
    *   Woman puts man or sensuality in the place of God
    *   The fundamental equality of the communion of persons is lost

    In addition there are other consequences that affect the roles of man and woman in society. For example:
    *   Man must "toil" for his living and Woman gives birth in "pain"
    *   continued discrimination against women and degradation of any man who discriminates

3. In Genesis, after the fall from grace by Adam and Eve, God offers a foreshadowing of the ultimate victory over sin which will come about through the gift of a savior, Jesus Christ. Integral to both the fall and the restoration of the human race are women — first Eve, then Mary. In both accounts, there is reference to "the Woman."

    Q. How are Eve and Mary similar? How do they differ?

    A. Both women are referred to as "Mother of the living." With Eve, her motherhood was physical since we attribute our place in the human race to her. Mary's motherhood was unique in that she gave birth to the God-man, and, from the Cross Jesus gave her to all of us as a spiritual mother. Having given birth to the One Who was "the firstborn of many brothers," her acceptance of God's plan makes eternal life possible by the work of her Son.

    The difference between these women is in the way they obeyed God. Eve was tempted by the serpent and chose to separate herself from the plan of God, introducing sin into the world. Mary rejected such a choice, receiving God into her womb, nurturing Him, following Him, suffering with Him, and ultimately crushing the head of that very serpent who had tricked Eve. In the words of the document, "Mary [is] the full revelation of all that is included in the biblical word 'woman:' a revelation commensurate with the mystery of the Redemption. Mary means ... a return to that 'beginning' in which one finds the 'woman' as she was intended to be in creation, and therefore in the eternal mind of God: in the bosom of the Most Holy Trinity. Mary is 'the new beginning' of *the dignity and vocation of women*, of each and every woman (11).

4. "*In Mary, Eve discovers* the nature of the true dignity of woman, of feminine humanity. This discovery must continually reach the heart of every woman and shape her vocation and her life" (11).

    Q. How are the following virtues exemplified by Mary in her vocation: humility; receptivity; joy; courage; and faith.

    A. Many answers are possible, for example: in her *Magnificat* (*Lk* 1:46-55), Mary attributes her goodness to her Creator and not herself; she receives the Child from the Holy Spirit simply because it is the will of God; doing the will of God is her joy — regardless of the hardship it may entail; she embraced her vocation despite the dire predictions of suffering that Simeon and Anna foretold; Mary trusted in the plan of God, not having any idea how it would come about because — having studied the Scriptures all her life — she trusted that God was true to His promises.

5. Q. How does the Holy Father caution the "women's rights" movement in seeking to restore equality?

A. There is need for conversion from sin and restoration to the equality and mutuality originally desired by God (10). The ultimate means is provided by God Himself in sending His only Son. Jesus heals us. The Pope reminds us that we must "safeguard the truth about the unity of the two," the "specific diversity and personal originality of man and woman."

Concern for women's rights is just. However, in seeking liberation from male domination, women must not adopt male characteristics contrary to their own feminine "originality." Women trying to be like men will "deform" their "essential richness." *Men and women are equal and complementary.*

The qualities of femininity are not less than those of masculinity, but they are different. A woman will find fulfillment by embracing the gifts of femininity; and a man, those of masculinity.

6. Q. Is there any hope in the face of the catastrophic sin and division spoken of in Questions 1 & 2?

A. After original sin, God's response was to promise a Redeemer (*Gn* 3:15). Sin was definitively defeated through the cooperation of Mary with her divine Son, Jesus Christ. Evil will continue to be overcome through a struggle in which woman holds a key place.

In John Paul II's *Letter to Women* he writes, "Women will increasingly play a part in the solution of the serious problems of the future: leisure time, the quality of life, migration, social services, euthanasia, drugs, health care, the ecology, etc. In all these areas a greater presence of women in society will prove most valuable, for it will help to manifest the contradictions present when society is organized solely according to the criteria of efficiency and productivity, and it will force systems to be redesigned in a way which favors the processes of humanization which mark the 'civilization of love.'"[6]

We see that woman will make an expanding impact on society by fulfilling her vocation to be a help or complement to man. Further on in that *Letter*, the Pope writes, "It is only through the duality of the masculine and the feminine that the human finds full realization."[7] This "full realization" is in God's plan and will transform society, building the Kingdom of Christ here on earth. The ultimate temptation to women

---

[6] *Letter to Women*, 4.

[7] *Ibid.* 7.

is to fight their degradation by adopting masculine models of behavior and trying to "beat men at their own game." The sign of contradiction in our faith is that God intends for the "feminine genius" to reflect the ways that the Woman can crush the head of the serpent, helping restore original unity.

7.   Q. **What is my place in this struggle? Do I make an impact in my sphere of influence?**
     A. Answers will vary.

SESSION FIVE

Mulieris Dignitatem
Articles 12-16

Jesus Christ

1. This session recalls women in the New Testament. It reflects upon the relationships Jesus had with women and what we can learn from them about the dignity and vocation of women.

    Q. In what ways did Jesus' attitude toward women reveal that the traditions operate contrary to the "ethos" of creation?

    A. Jesus did not share the attitude of His contemporaries. He was a "promoter of women's true dignity and vocation" and this often shocked and surprised people, even His disciples. He protested whatever offended the dignity of women — which included the Jewish customs surrounding divorce, putting away wives, shunning sinners, and categorizing certain women as unclean. Christ always spoke and acted in opposition to the tradition of discriminating against and dominating women while upholding life-long marriage as a reflection of the original unity between man and woman (cf. *Mt* 19). "His words and works always express the respect and honor due to women" (*MD*, 13) and to this end, He revealed to them the mysteries of the Kingdom, talking directly and lovingly to them with understanding.

2. **Q. Which are the key messages of the meeting of Jesus with the woman caught in adultery? (14; *Jn.* 8:3-11)**

    A. "Jesus enters into the concrete and historical situation of women, weighed down by the inheritance of sin" (*MD*, 14). One way this inheritance of sin is expressed is by the "habitual discrimination against women in favor of men." This attitude was also rooted in women.

    - Jesus evokes an awareness of sin in the men who accuse the woman. He knows people's hearts. This is powerfully acknowledged by the Pope: women are often abandoned, exposed to the public, while men, who are just as guilty, hide. Woman often pays for her own sin all alone, utterly abandoned by the man who also sins.

    - The Pope returns to his theme of "entrusting." In the beginning — the original unity — the Creator entrusted man and woman to each other to be a mutual gift.

    - Man must accept responsibility for his sin and for failure to respect and cherish woman. Man must look within his heart to purify his attitude toward woman, to see her as sister and bride and not as an object of exploitation and pleasure.

- Woman must be responsible for herself before man, finding in the teaching of Christ "their own subjectivity and dignity" (*MD*, 14).

3. **Q. What are some important points in the encounter between Jesus and the Samaritan woman? (15; *Jn*. 4:39-42)**

   A. Jesus liberated women with the truth about themselves.
   - Women felt loved by Jesus with an "eternal love," even if He confronted them with their sinfulness, as in the case of the Samaritan woman. Jesus knows she is a sinner and discusses her situation with her. He speaks of God's love for her, of the Spirit, and of true worship.
   - Jesus even reveals to her that He is the Messiah. He entrusts divine truths to women as well as to men. They have equal dignity and vocation as children of God. He speaks to her of the things of God, thus recognizing and restoring her intellectual and spiritual powers. This is an event without precedent: that a *woman,* and, what is more, a sinful woman becomes a disciple of Christ. Indeed, she proclaims Christ to the inhabitants of Samaria, so that they too receive Him with faith.

4. **Q. Considering the story of the Samaritan woman, do you see a pattern similar to Christ's other encounters with women?**

   A. The women follow this process of becoming disciples. In some way, they always bring others to Christ. They:
   - listen
   - learn
   - understand
   - believe
   - proclaim to others

5. **Q. Why is Jesus' conversation with Martha in *Jn*. 11:21-27 "one of the most important in the Gospels"?**

   A. It reveals the deep capacity for spiritual truths within women and their response of faith. Here we see the "feminine" response: understanding in the mind and conversion in the heart. *Woman gives her whole being to another.* Faith in Christ is not just intellectual. It also requires a response of the heart that brings a lasting conversion and commitment. It was this loving and faithful devotion of heart that gave the women the strength to remain at the foot of the Cross.

6. **Q. What feminine quality does Mary Magdalene reveal at the Resurrection?**

   A. Mary Magdalene and the other women at the empty tomb show a deep sensitivity to the mystery and mission of Christ. They do not abandon Him even in death. They intuitively know "there is more" to Christ, even if they cannot articulate it. Although women may be abandoned (as the woman caught in adultery), *in their finest moments they do not abandon those entrusted to them.* They express the fidelity of God who compares Himself to a mother who can never forget the child of her womb (*Is.* 49:14-15). It is part of woman's nature to accept the gift of life no matter what difficulty it entails (*MD*,14). This acceptance is not always easy and automatic. It sometimes takes time and wrestling with God's will.

   Note that Mary is the "first to bear witness to Him before the Apostles." She is the "apostle of the Apostles."

7. **Q. What are some of the ways the Spirit at Pentecost confirms the equality of men and women?**

   A. Men and women both are:
   * created in God's image and likeness
   * capable of receiving divine truth and love in the Holy Spirit
   * receive the Spirit's salvific and sanctifying visit
   * called to prophesy to the "mighty works of God" (cf. *Joel* 3:1)

8. **Q. Do you find yourself relating to any of the women in the Gospels? In what way?**

   A. The responses will vary.

9. Pope John Paul II was himself the greatest and most visible prophet in recent history along with the life testimony of Blessed Mother Teresa. However, we are all called to be prophets within our own families and communities. We must stand for the truth — witness to it — through our words and actions.

   Q. Who do you know in your own communities who are doing this in a heroic way? How can you also be a more effective prophet?

   A. Answers may include pro-life activists, neighbors, those suffering illness heroically, anyone defending the truths of the Catholic faith and going "against the grain."

SESSION SIX

Mulieris Dignitatem
Articles 17-19

Motherhood

1. "In order to share in this 'vision' [the true vocation of women], we must . . . seek a deeper understanding of the truth about the human person" (*MD*, 18).
    Q. How does the Pope define the human person?
    A. "The human person is the only being in the world which God willed and created for its own sake." The person is a subject with free will and has been created for communion with others. We see the same theme in *Gaudium et Spes* which states, "man, who is the only creature on earth which God willed for itself, cannot fully find himself except through a sincere gift of himself."[8] In his book, *Be Not Afraid*, Pope John Paul II states, "Man affirms himself most completely by giving himself. This is the fulfillment of the law of love" (from the chapter on human rights). The Gospel is our record of the giving exemplified by Jesus Himself. It is the model for our life.

2. **Q. Why is openness to persons an important quality for woman and motherhood?**
    A. Openness to the other is the hallmark of woman since physiologically she has been created to be receptive. The very act of self-giving that a woman shows to her husband in the marital embrace calls for complete openness, receptivity, surrender. This is not a passive attitude, but an active response of love by which the woman freely gives herself to another. When conception takes place, an interior openness welcomes, nurtures, cares for, protects the spark of life within. The child within her womb is truly another person in the image and likeness of God. The child is the "other" with whom the mother relates in a secret, yet profound way.
    This femininity pattern is to be lived at all times on a pure and chaste level with others in her life. The Pope speaks of a "special communion with the mystery of life" (*MD*, 18) which women share when they embrace their vocation to love. Many scientific studies have been completed, but true motherhood is not merely a biological fact, but a personal act. Motherhood is an opportunity for a woman to give herself

---

[8] *Gaudium et spes*, 24.

totally to another — physically, emotionally, spiritually. When woman is not open to the other she thwarts her own nature, dignity and vocation.

Mary's "fiat" — "Let it be done" — is a sincere gift of self and a readiness to give one's self and accept new life.

3. The Pope clearly explains how "the woman's motherhood constitutes a special 'part' in our shared parenthood." The woman "pays" dearly and directly for new life, "which literally absorbs the energies of her body and soul." Hence, the man owes her a special debt of gratitude and respect. The Holy Father further states, "The man — even with all his sharing in parenthood — always remains 'outside' the process of pregnancy and the baby's birth; in many ways he has to learn his own 'fatherhood' from the mother." Parents must work together, but it is the mother who lays the foundation for family and forms a new personality in the child (*MD*, 18, paragraph 6).

Q. How is a woman's attitude towards men, beginning with her own husband, indicative of how he is received within the family? His circle?

A. A woman should respect her husband as protector and provider through her attitude and words. His children will learn love and respect for him if their mother shows them how. There are many practical ways to develop the father relationship in the day-to-day happenings in the household. The father can be a strong moral figure in the home with the support of his wife. He has ample opportunity to teach the children all of the values of courage, perseverance, generosity, chastity, patience, temperance, etc., if he is encouraged and affirmed by his wife. Some examples are to speak of his courage and to put our husbands first next to God in our lives.

4. Q. How can we combat the ubiquitous negative image of men in the media?

A. The first step is not to participate in jokes and stories that make fun of men, and to avoid conversations that degrade masculinity in general. If our family members see and hear such things, we can take them aside and say that men deserve respect and remind them of the good qualities in the men we know. Understanding that some men have reneged on their responsibilities, we have to give others the opportunity to live up to their potential and to encourage them in every possible way that we know they can.

5. Q. Can you give examples of women who have paid a "high price" for

their children? Or men who have been keenly aware of sacrifices made by their wives?

A. One example is St. Gianna Beretta Molla who died in 1962 at the age of 39. She had been a medical doctor and mother of four children. While pregnant with her fourth child, the doctors discovered she had uterine cancer. She refused the recommended surgery that would have killed her baby. "If you must decide between me and the child, do not hesitate: choose the child — I insist ⟨...⟩ a died a week after giving birth to a dau⟨...⟩o was present at her mother's canonizatio⟨...⟩ically gave up her life for her child.

Slave women in the ante-bellum ⟨...⟩r their motherhood, working hard throug⟨...⟩ their young children in dire circumstance⟨...⟩gainst their will, and many times losing the⟨...⟩ims of others. Countless stories are told of ⟨...⟩ove — even at the high risk of loss. They g⟨...⟩ith no personal return except heartache.

> • The earliest stage of motherhood is pure self-gift without recieving anything from the child in return.

6.

Q. How does motherhood make a woman more attentive to other people in general? Do you have personal experiences to share?

A. The unique openness to the child hidden within the womb before birth and afterwards, as the child develops, enables the woman to appreciate the uniqueness of each person. She learns to give her attention to others, even in the littlest things. In the beginning, motherhood is pure self-gift with no active response, not even a smile or recognition from the newborn. All the joy is in the giving. Later, as the baby develops and begins to respond, she enjoys the precious and inimitable return of love. The life of that child should offer years of give and take, for the ultimate benefit of both.

7.

Q. How does the motherhood of every woman share in the New Covenant of Christ's death and resurrection? What does this mean in my life?

A. Motherhood is not only physical, but spiritual, like Mary's motherhood of all humanity. Motherhood in the New Covenant involves:
- listening to the Word of God
- safeguarding that Word
- being willing to share in the Paschal Mystery

We must study the Word of God, hear it, make sure that those around us are able to receive the truth therein. Just as the Incarnate Son would have no flesh without the "Fiat" of Mary and His redemptive sacrifice could not have occurred. Our Yes to the other and our support of fatherhood will provide an essential bridge to God the Father that all require for salvation.

Paul Evdokimov wrote that maternity is the sacramental character inscribed within the very being of woman. "To protect the world of men as a mother and to purify it as a virgin, giving this world a soul, her soul: This is the vocation of every woman, religious, celibate or spouse."[9]

8. **Discuss how women share in the Paschal Mystery.**

A. Women share in that Mystery through their suffering — and to love in a fallen world means to suffer. John Paul II speaks of those who are suffering in loneliness; suffering through the pains of their children; the sufferings of being wronged or exploited, among countless other examples. These sufferings are to be placed at the foot of the Cross. The Holy Father compares the pain and joy of childbirth to the pain and joy of the Paschal Mystery. Note that the Holy Father has called for the canonization of married men and women who have achieved great holiness through fidelity to their vocation.

---

[9] Paul Evdokimov, *Sacrement de l'Amour: Le mystere conjugal a la lumiere de la tradition ortodoxe*, Paris, 1962, p. 42.

Mulieris Dignitatem
Articles 20-22

Virginity

1. Jesus describes "a voluntary celibacy, chosen for the sake of the Kingdom of heaven, in view of man's eschatological vocation to union with God." This comes not only from the choice of the individual but by means of a special grace from God as part of the call.
    Q. What are the two most important aspects of the celibate vocation?
    A. The first point is that the faithful celibate is an "eschatological sign" for others, meaning he or she is a signpost for what awaits us in heaven. There will be no marrying or giving in marriage, because all souls will embrace God as their ultimate end. The consecrated woman who is espoused to God is a special sign of that perfect union and reminds us that God will provide total happiness in the world to come.

    The second point is that virginity for the Kingdom allows the celibate to focus all his energy, all his devotion, and all his activity towards building the Kingdom of God.

2. The Pope writes, "In the teaching of Christ, motherhood is connected with virginity, but also distinct from it."
    Q. What are some of the similarities and some of the differences of these two vocations?
    A. Both are a calling of life, voluntarily and freely chosen — one to an earthly union, the other to a union with God in heaven. Spousal love in both forms is the "sincere gift of one person" to the other. Both vocations are gifts from God, and in both we receive special graces so that the woman is faithful, open, receptive, and nurturing to souls. In virginity, spousal love is extended toward Jesus and His mission to build the kingdom of God. According to St. Paul in *1 Cor* 7:32-35, the married woman's primary responsibility is towards the needs of her family.

    Love for Christ impels the virgin to love all — each and every person. Blessed Mother Teresa of Calcutta is an example of virginal love pouring itself out to others for the good of body and soul. In human marriage, spousal love between husband and wife give children a tremendous amount of sense of security and well-being so that they can recognize the voice of God when they hear it. In this way, the vocations are intertwined and depend on each other for the good of souls and the Church.

Mary was privileged to live both simultaneously and is the most perfect example of each.

3. **Q. How can a woman dedicated to God by the vow of chastity exercise her full personhood?**

   A. Contrary to the ideas of the world today, the deeper understanding of this beautiful gift of human sexuality is truly a means of exercising the fullness of personhood (*MD*, 21) for:
   - In choosing to make this vow, a woman is acting freely as a person created in God's image and likeness.
   - She gives the "sincere gift of self" to God, to Christ as her Spouse.
   - This gift of self is a response to Jesus' gift of Himself to her in love. Hence, it is a mutual gift.
   - This spiritual union is fruitful in obtaining grace for others.
   - It is also manifested in concrete concern for other people, especially for those in need.
   - Gospel virginity is not simply a matter of being unmarried or single. It is a choice of giving love in a total and undivided manner, analogous to marriage.

4. **Q. How do the evangelical counsels of consecrated life (poverty, chastity, and obedience) each provide a means of witnessing to the larger world that has forgotten God to a large extent?**

   A. The evangelical counsels draw attention to the "radicalism of the Gospel" (*MD*, 20), which requires tremendous trust in the promises of God. The poverty of life begins by detaching the soul from the material distractions of the world, and calls her to depend on God completely to satisfy the most basic needs. Chastity allows the consecrated soul to imitate both Jesus and Mary, and the subsequent purity brings about "an integral faith, firm hope, and a sincere charity" (*MD* ,22). Living a joyful obedience causes the chosen soul to lay aside her own will, her own pride, and her own ego so that she becomes a fitting instrument for the plan of God as He reveals it through her approved statutes, constitutions, and prayerful superiors — themselves subject to God's call.

5. **Q. Does this explanation of virginity help to understand why the Church values celibacy for priests?**

   A. A person finds fulfillment by the "sincere gift of self" to another. We cannot give ourselves totally to more than one person. Just as a married man gives the total gift of himself to his wife, so the priest gives the total gift of self in a spousal way to Holy Mother Church, in imitation of the Bridegroom. Closely identified and conformed with Christ, the priest is wedded to the Church. His entire life is spent for Her, and he would lay down his life if necessary to safeguard the flock.

It should be noted that the celibacy of Catholic priests is a discipline and not a dogma. The Church has the prerogative to change it should the need arise, but the Magisterium has stated clearly that the value of the sacrifice and witness is so valuable that it is unlikely to be changed.

6. Q. **What are some practical ways to show support for those who are called to embrace the evangelical counsels? Where are these men and women found in your local area?**

A. One way is by speaking highly of the vocations to the priestly and religious life. Invite priests and religious to your home for dinner or special occasions. Share stories of the saints with others. Give an example of chastity (to which everyone is called). Make sure that children are reminded that they could be called to either marriage or a celibate vocation, as a priest or religious.

Besides the local parishes, research and discuss the convents and monasteries nearby and consider dropping in for a visit if appropriate.

SESSION EIGHT

Mulieris Dignitatem
Articles 23-27

The Church — the Bride of Christ

1. John Paul II, in his theology of the body, returned to the fundamental truth about the relationship between God and His creation. Marriage is described as the "primordial sacrament," meaning that it lies at the very foundation of our being — since man, in the image and likeness of God, is made for intimate communion with God and others — thus he is completed by spousal love.

    Q. Explain "spousal love." How is it applied to God and His people?

    A. Spousal love describes the mutual self-giving of man and woman in marriage, the "unity of the two." A recurring theme in the Old Testament is that the covenant between God and Israel is like a marriage bond (cf. *Hos* 2:16-18; *Jer* 2:2; *Is* 54:4-8, 10). Unfaithfulness to God and idolatry are described in the Old Testament as adultery. This theme continues in the New Testament with Christ as the Bridegroom and the Church — the new people of God — as His Bride. This spousal theme running through all of the Scriptures is very important and cannot be easily dismissed. It reveals God's relationship with us and also gives greater depth and meaning to the human institution of marriage.

2. **Q. What are the two dimensions of the analogy of spousal love (*MD*, 23)?**

    A. The "great mystery" of spousal love has two dimensions. The first dimension is the human reality in the daily, concrete lives of men and women united in marriage. The second dimension is symbolic on a spiritual level. The spousal union of love between husband and wife joins the human with the divine, because the analogy is human, but the love that it expresses is divine — the essence of God Himself.

3. **Q. If spousal love is the backdrop to creation, then what does that say about women, who are called to be icons of the Bride?**

    A. The "great mystery" into which this document delves is rich, and deep and profound. Scripture shows it to us through the writing of Saint Paul to the church at Corinth, "I feel a divine jealousy for you, for I betrothed you to Christ to present you as a pure bride to her one husband" (2 *Cor* 11:2). He later writes to the church at Ephesus, "*Christ loved the*

Church and gave himself up for her" (*Eph* 5:25). If the bride is worth the shedding of the Blood of the Lamb, then she should try to live as a pure and holy spouse in gratitude for His great gift. In a fascinating way, while the whole Church is espoused to Jesus as His bride, it is women — as women — who are called in a deeper way to give witness to the Bride by their natural feminine gifts.

It is important to note that Jesus the Bridegroom is perfect (being divine) and the Church (as Spotless Bride) is called to perfection. Those who imitate each (as icons of the bride and bridegroom) are certainly fallible, but should always keep before their eyes the perfection to which they aspire. Defects in the creatures should not indict the perfect plan of God, which has been given to us as paradigm or model.

4. **Q. What do we mean by saying Mary is a "figure" or "type" of the Church?**

A. Mary Immaculate, who was preserved from all sin by the grace of God, shows us how we are to respond to the life-giving love of the Bridegroom. She has lived and attained what the Church is called to become and thus provides a model and image of the Church, as both virgin and mother (*MD*, 22). Jesus said the Church becomes a mother to Him by "hearing, and keeping the word of God" (cf. *Lk* 8:19-21). As mother, the Church gives spiritual birth through the Holy Spirit — receiving life as Mary did at the Annunciation; then nurturing that life, teaching and protecting her spiritual children through safeguarding the truth in season and out.

The Church is virgin insofar as she remains whole-heartedly and steadfastly committed to her Spouse, Jesus Christ. Mary was the perfect model of charity, of faithfully fulfilling the will of God, and of steadfastness, remaining with Jesus to the end. She stood beneath the Cross, and subsequently forgave and embraced as children those who had crucified her Son. She loves each one of us and points the way to Jesus through the sacraments of the Church.

5. In this pivotal time in the history of the Church, so much attention is being paid to women and their vocation. The Holy Father concludes this chapter by saying that no one can have an "adequate hermeneutic" of humanity without "appropriate reference to what is 'feminine'" (*MD*, 22, para.3).

Q. Why does the Pope say the feminine becomes the symbol of all humanity (25)?

A. In revelation (Old and New Testament), God and Christ are represented as the Bridegroom, a masculine symbol; and humanity, the people, is always symbolized as the Bride. God always takes the initiative and humanity responds. Woman, by nature is a bride, which allows her to more naturally embody this icon. All people (men and women) express a feminine quality in their relationship to God. This is done when a person is receptive to the gift of Christ's love and tries to respond with the gift of self.

Men are called to imitate the Bridegroom in their daily lives, Who "is the model and pattern of all human love, men's love in particular," but ultimately everyone has to learn to receive the will of God and respond accordingly.

6. **Q. Why does Christ call only men to be priests?**

A. The Eucharist is the "marriage covenant" where Christ gives Himself for His bride the Church (*MD*, 25, paragraph 4). It is thus fitting for a man to stand in the person of Christ *in persona Christi* as the Bridegroom. This nuptial relationship of God and the Church is a revealed truth (a truth we can't know by human reason alone). God's creation of man and woman as a unity in His image and likeness is not only on the physical level, but also on the spiritual. It permeates humanity's relationship with the Trinity.

All recent papal exhortations have emphasized that a male priesthood is essential and rooted in the Church's divine and fundamental constitution, as well as its theological anthropology. (This is a technical way of saying all that has been pointed out so far in *Mulieris Dignitatem*.) The heart of the Eucharist, for which the priesthood is necessary, is the Pascal mystery in which the Blood of Jesus is poured out. "The Eucharist makes present and realizes anew in a sacramental manner the redemptive act of Christ" (*MD*, 26). There is a profound nuptial union taking place in the sanctuary, which would be rendered sterile with a female attempting to stand *in persona Christi*. The feminine model is the Church, which receives the gift of the Bridegroom in order to bear spiritual fruit.

7. **Q. How do all the baptized share in the "universal priesthood" of Christ?**

A. By our baptism we share in Christ's mission of priest, prophet and king (*MD*, 27). Pope John Paul II discusses this at great length in his first encyclical, *Redemptor Hominis*. All the baptized share in Christ's priesthood by receiving the ability to offer God worship and praise. "Present your bodies as a living sacrifice, holy and acceptable to God, which is your spiritual worship" (*Rm* 12:1).

The baptized witness to their faith in Christ. Through the Holy Spirit dwelling within our hearts, every moment of our day can become a "sacrifice of praise" to God. Think of all your daily actions as part of this "sacrifice of praise."

This universal or royal priesthood of personal holiness and the gift of self to Christ in love as a bride helps describe the essence of the Church. The Holy father writes, "And holiness is measured according to the 'great mystery' in which the Bride responds with the gift of love to the gift of the Bridegroom" (*MD*, 27).

The "ministerial" priesthood differs and is characterized by service to the Church. The ministerial priesthood acts in the person of Christ in a special way through the sacraments.

Mulieris Dignitatem
Articles 28-30

The Greatest of These Is Love

1. Q. **What does the Pope say is "decisive for the dignity of women"?**
    A. Woman is the first creature in whom the "order of love" takes root (*MD*, 29). That is to say, woman is the first to be loved and to love in return. This is a very great dignity indeed; a profound way in which she images the Trinity and also represents humanity.

    God's intimate life is love (*1 Jn* 4:16), the love of Three Persons, the very essence of the God-head. The Holy Spirit is love personified. Love is a gift to human persons "poured into our hearts by the Holy Spirit" (*Rm* 5:5). In the scriptural images of Genesis and Ephesians, God creates woman as a mutual companion to man. The Man/Bridegroom loves the Woman/Bride. "It is she who receives love, in order to love in return." It is essential to understand the order and primacy of love to appreciate the profound dignity and vocation of women. Woman is a person of love no matter where she lives or if she is married or single, because her feminine gifts are to be used in all interpersonal relationships (*MD*, 29, paragraph 5).

2. Q. **What is the "prophetic" character of women in their femininity?**
    A. Woman's femininity is prophetic because it proclaims that every person is made for love and becomes fully oneself by loving in return (*MD*, 29). "Woman can only find herself by giving love to others" (*MD*, 30, paragraph 1). This applies to all people, but women clearly manifest the reality of this truth.

3. Q. **How is the Virgin Mother of God the highest expression of this prophetic role?**
    A. Mary as the *woman par excellence* of the Scriptures exemplifies that every person is uniquely loved by God (*MD*, 29). By her fiat, she says "yes" to God with her whole being. Mary reveals the awesome power of human free will because God awaited her decision to become the Mother of His Son, and in her acquiescence, she "[reveals] the true order of love which constitutes woman's own vocation" (*MD*, 30).

    Mary as the Mother of the Savior, the New Eve, stands at the center of the struggle between good and evil. Her "yes" opens the gates of salvation for the whole world (cf. *Letter to Women*, 10), and thus restored the relationship between God and His creatures, giving them a means by which they could respond to His love.

4. Each woman is called to repeat the words of the Blessed Mother: "Behold the handmaid of the Lord. Let it be done to me according to your word." By now, we can understand better the ways in which the secular world struggles against femininity, motherhood, or patriarchy because of various misconceptions — imagined or deliberate.

    Q. How does Mary's role in salvation apply to women? To you in particular?

    A. Answers will vary, but recall that woman, because she is at the heart of love, is at the heart of the world (*MD*, 30). The struggle for salvation continues to be linked to the role of woman. Woman, like and with Mary, is at the heart of the struggle against Evil, which wants to devour the "child," all those lovingly entrusted to her care. Each woman's decision to say "yes" to God's will and not accept the seductions of the world is crucial for the future of civilization.

5. The Holy Father associates women with "entrustment" (*MD*, 30).

    Q. How does the Pope relate entrustment to the universal and fundamental vocation of women?

    A. "God entrusts the human being to her in a special way" (*MD*, 30, paragraph 4). We are all entrusted to one another in a general way by the fact that we are persons needing loving relationships to find fulfillment and meaning in our lives. But the entrustment of persons to women is of particular significance for her unique vocation. Where each woman is entrusted with the task of revealing God's love to particular persons by their spiritual or physical maternity, women look to Mary as a model, since she was entrusted with the entire human race. A woman's moral and spiritual strength comes from her awareness of her vocation of being entrusted by God with the good of humanity (*MD*, 30, paragraph 5 & 6).

6. **If a woman's primary vocation is to love, how does this become practically manifest in the various arenas in which she works, lives, and collaborates?**

    A. Woman's fundamental vocation is to care for, love, and foster unity and relationships among persons. In a sense, her role is analogous to the Holy Spirit the bond of love between the Father and the Son. Woman's vocation is to foster love, divine life, conversion and growth. This basic vocation will be expressed in different ways according to the particular vocations and circumstances of each woman.

In his *Letter to Women*, the Holy Father, speaking of progress "measured according to the criteria of science and technology," tells us, "Much more important is the social and ethical dimension which deals with human relations and spiritual values. In this area, which often develops in an inconspicuous way beginning with the daily relationships between people, especially within the family, society certainly owes much to the "genius of women."[10]

Note that in the opening paragraphs of this letter the Pope has thanked women for their presence and action "in every area of life — social, economic, cultural, artistic, and political." Now, in article 9, he expresses "particular appreciation to those women who are involved in the various areas of education extending well beyond the family: nurseries, schools, universities, social service agencies, parishes, association and movements. . . . In this work they [women] exhibit a kind of affective, cultural, and spiritual motherhood which has inestimable value for the development of individuals and the future of society."[11]

---

[10] *Letter to Women*, 9.

[11] *Ibid.*

Mulieris Dignitatem
Articles 30-31

1. In the first lesson of this study and the opening paragraph of the document, the following quote was highlighted from the closing message of the Second Vatican Council:

    "The hour is coming, in fact has come, when the vocation of women is being acknowledged in its fullness, the hour in which women acquire in the world an influence, an effect and a power never hitherto achieved. That is why, at this moment when the human race is undergoing so deep a transformation, women imbued with a spirit of the Gospel can do so much to aid humanity in not falling."[12]

    Q. What is the "feminine genius" of which the Holy Father speaks and which he believes will transform the world? (*MD*, 30)

    A. Women after the example of Mary (redeemed by Christ and growing in sanctity in the Holy Spirit) respond to God's call and thus become channels of His grace for the world. The Pope has made some extraordinary statements about the importance, influence and "power" of women. He says, "Christ looks to them [women] for the accomplishment of the 'royal priesthood'" (*MD*, 30).

    Women are called by God to be a "support and source of spiritual strength for other people" (*MD*, 30). To be instruments of His grace, they need a deep prayer life and union with God. Woman's unique contribution is greatly needed today in the world, for where it is lacking, there is a "loss of sensitivity ... for what is essentially human." Women, cooperating with the grace of Christ, intuitively know the path for restoring the image and likeness in humans; of enabling others to feel they are loved and belong; that someone cares, listens and understands them. The deepest realities people are hungering for correspond to the gifts and "genius" of women.

2. **Q. The Pope calls women to use their moral and spiritual strength for the good of the human person, so that others might know love. What is the price of fidelity to this mission to love?**

    A. We are asked to offer the sacrifice of our very selves; to submit to the "obedience of faith;" to carry our cross daily; to get rid of anything that

---

[12] *Address of Pope Paul VI to Women* (December 8, 1965).

would hinder the full presence of God in our lives. As we saw earlier, St. Paul wrote, "Present your bodies as a living sacrifice, holy and acceptable to God, which is your spiritual worship" (*Rm* 12:1).

- It means to live fully as women; to pour ourselves out in loving concern for others; to foster, nourish and defend life.
- It means to offer our lives totally to God that we may be transformed more fully into icons of the Bride, Holy Mother Church, responding to the call of the Bridegroom. Make a morning offering prayer, and be aware of Christ at your side during the events of the day.
- It means to become love. Reject selfishness, bitterness, envy, unkindness, impatience and anything else that keeps you from becoming love to all in your life. Of course loving in a fallen world implies suffering.

3. **Q.** **The Holy Father makes a brief reference to "the mystery of woman" (*MD*, 31) without expanding on that term. Given the backdrop of the entire document, what do you think he had in mind?**

    A. It is hard to say definitively, but educated guesses would take into consideration the way that masculinity and femininity are each reflections of God: fundamentally equal, and yet distinct in important ways. One would look at the way that God generates life — concerning both our physical existence and our spiritual destiny — and the essential part that maternity plays in His plan. It could also be a reflection of the hierarchies of the created universe, in that woman was created last — as some say the crown of creation. Despite her humility, her potential to be oppressed, and the danger that her physical vulnerability poses, she is first in the order of love and essential to giving flesh to spiritual realities.

4. The wording of this document shows respect and support for women in so many settings — those who are single, married, consecrated, religious, professionals, "perfect," "weak," well-supported, struggling, or abandoned. Overall, it stresses gratitude to women for their fidelity, their heroic action, and their courageous witness in many walks of life.

    Q. **What, then, is the common thread that the Church wants to promote about authentic femininity?**

    A. With the physiological designation of "female" comes the simple, but universal call to receive God's love, to receive the human persons entrusted to her with the dignity that is due, and to be an icon of the Bride, the Church. The Magisterium has never offered a "job description" for women, a narrowing of gifts that shackle them to the home, or denied them education or legal rights. The Church has always understood that the equal dignity of women was a refreshing reality that Jesus restored — first because He chose to be born of a woman, and then He engaged them as full partners in His mission. When He was pierced on the cross, and the Church — the paradigm for women — was born from His side, He brought her forth as a Spouse washed in His blood, familiar with suffering, and dedicated to her Savior. Each woman should link her suffering to that redemptive act, rejoice in being called to bear His love to the world, and radiate the life-giving joy that union with Christ offers.

5. Q. **After having reflected so long now on the essence of womanhood, what unique gifts can women bring to the world — through the workplace, the classroom, in the political arena, in civic associations — combining professionalism with their femininity?**

   A. Answers will vary. Women are completely capable of contributing to many spheres and should use their skills for the ultimate good of the human person. Even jobs that don't require human interaction (or have very little of it) must be couched in the context of the value it provides, and all relationships with co-workers should be based on mutual respect and sincere concern for their well-being. Women must fight two temptations: one, that they relinquish their femininity and become harsh or cold in order to be taken seriously; or two, that they undermine professionalism by being too distracted by the human element. With prayer and forethought, each woman can find a middle ground that allows her to use her "feminine genius" in these settings.

6. Q. **Review the attacks on authentic femininity and the ways that it is misunderstood in the world today. Focus specifically in the way that motherhood is described by the secular world.**

   A. There are many angles of attack:
   - Radical feminism wants to eradicate the differences between men and women;
   - The sexual revolution wants to undermine purity and encourage promiscuity in men and women;
   - Abortion and contraception are promoted as salvation for women, who would otherwise suffer from unwanted pregnancies;
   - Many argue that motherhood is a form of control or "slavery" from which women have to be freed;
   - Children are considered economic liabilities that are more burdens than joys;

- Women are encouraged to work by being told that economic worth defines her as a person;
- Openness to life is discouraged as demeaning to women, who will be tied to the physical needs of others, undermining "self fulfillment;"
- Women are pitted against men in opposition, with claims that collaboration will only hurt women;
- The ministerial priesthood is pursued by some women who insist that it is the "path to power" rather than a sacrificial image of the Bridegroom;
- The world claims that freedom, autonomy and self-fulfillment will bring about more happiness than generous service.

7. You discover your gift by giving it; or in the words of Pope John Paul II, "woman finds herself by the sincere gift of herself to the other." The Holy Father also wrote in his *1995 World Day of Peace Message*, "When women are able fully to share their gifts with their families and the whole community, the very way in which society understands and organizes itself is improved" (*Message*, 4). The Pope is counting on women of the Church to be on the "front lines" ushering in the "civilization of love" in the Third Millennium.

   Q. Having reflected on your unique gifts or talents, what more will you do to share those gifts, to help usher in that "civilization of love"?

   A. Answers will vary.

References:

_____Paul Evdokimov, *"Sacrement de l'Amour: Le mystere conjugal a la lumiere de la tradition ortodoxe."* Paris. 1962, p. 42.

_____Joyce A. Little, *"The Significance of Mary for Women,"* Queen of Apostolate Series, Vol. III, 1989, (World Apostolate of Fatima, P.O. Box 976, Washington, NJ 07882), pp. 19, 24-25.

_____Rev. Arthur B. Calkins, *"Totus Tuus: John Paul's II's Program of Marian Consecration and Entrustment."* New Bedford, MA. Academy of the Immaculate, 1992 (P. O. Box 667, Valatie, NY 12184), pp. 231-232.

Leader's Evaluation - The Dignity and Vocation of Women

1. Did the Leader's Manual assist you in presenting the material?

2. How did your own experience in the program affect you personally?

3. How much preparation time did you need for each session?

4. In general, did the questions stimulate discussion?

5. Were the time and location of your group meetings appropriate?

6. Are you interested in leading another TOGETHER! group soon?

7. Who do you know that may be interested in starting a TOGETHER! group in the next year?

    Name: _____ Phone: _____-_____-_____

8. The following parish may be interested in starting TOGETHER! groups:

    Parish: _____ City: _____

    Contact: _____ Phone: _____-_____-_____

    Address: _____ City _____ Zip _____

    E-mail: _____ State: ___

9. The following is optional but provides us the means to notify you of upcoming programs:

    My Name: _____ My group location: _____

    E-mail: _____

    Please send the completed evaluation to the address on the other side of this page.

    Thank you! May God richly bless you!

    Paul and Libbie Sellors

Send to: **Together!**
3205 Roosevelt Street NE
St Anthony   MN   55418

Notes

Notes

Notes

Notes

Notes

Notes

Notes

CPSIA information can be obtained at www.ICGtesting.com
Printed in the USA
BVOW020131110213

312823BV00005B/89/P

9 781933 463117